Walter
the
Worrier

Also by this author:
Hooray for Henry
Everything I Do You Blame on Me!

Visit the website at:
www.waltertheworrier.com

ISBN-10: 1461090814
EAN-13: 9781461090816
LCCN: 2011905973

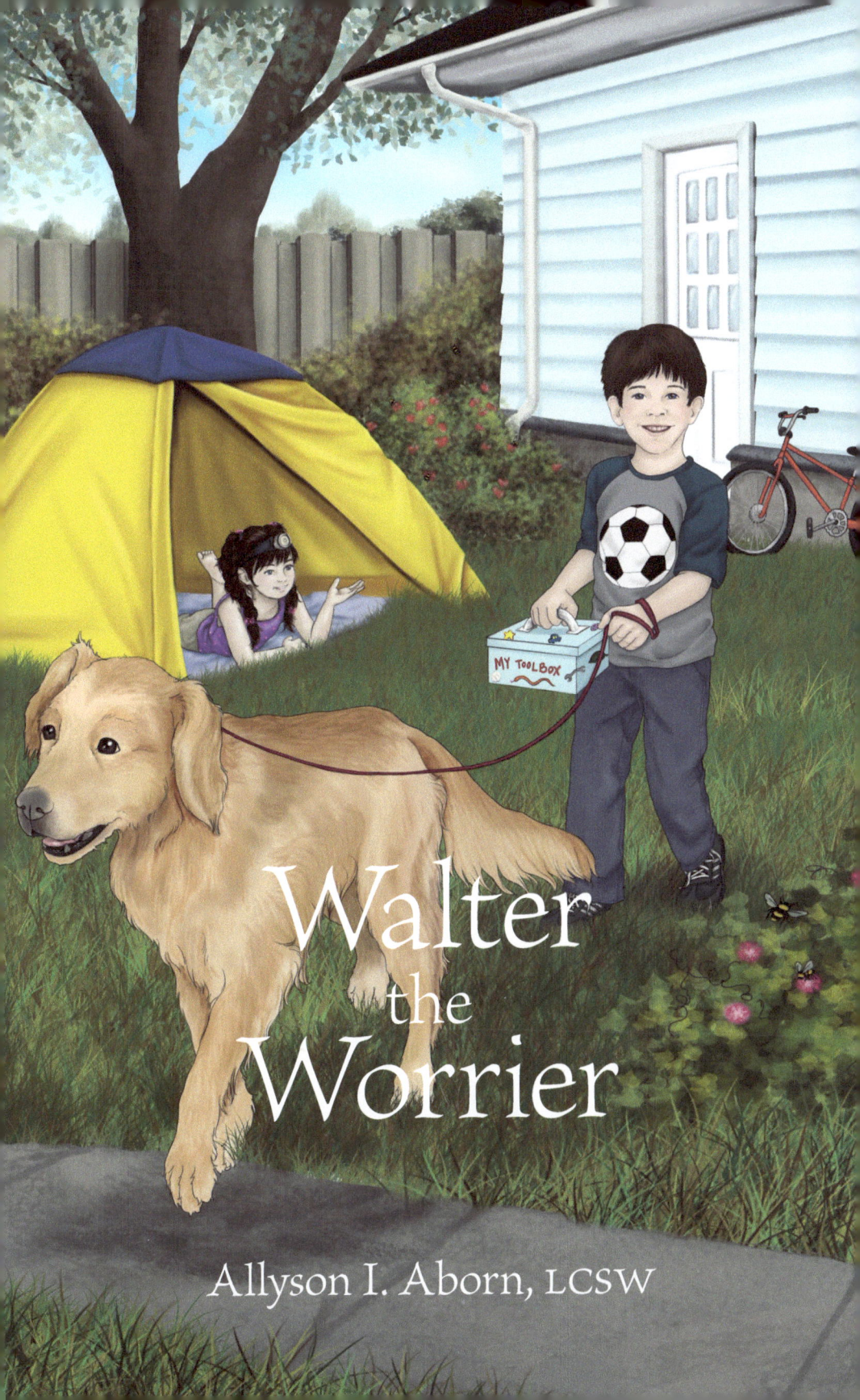

Walter the Worrier

Allyson I. Aborn, LCSW

For BBD
Who believes everything is possible

Introduction

PEOPLE WORRY. CHILDREN worry. Most children worry at various points in their childhood about typical developmental and social issues. It is also to be expected that certain traumatic events occurring in a child's life can engender an anxious reaction.

This book, however, focuses on children who are consumed by worry and live in a world of "what ifs". That world is rife with potential dangers. These children exaggerate risk and have an impaired sense of their ability to cope. They are tormented by issues that are not inherently problematic. Even when the etiology of the worry has a foundation in reality, their response is so excessive as to interfere with their ability to function.

These children can be driven to overcorrect for the possibility of harm to themselves and those close to them. Their families, as well as those who are involved with them in school and community, can be deeply affected by their relentless search for steadier ground.

Walter the Worrier tells the story of one such child, a child whose life has been significantly compromised by the perceived dangers of the world around him. The quality of his family's life is equally constricted as they attempt to make the world a safe place for him. Walter is unable to enjoy the more typical developmental pleasures of childhood because he is so consumed with his attempts to control his environment. The tensions that ensue for him and for his family are daunting.

How Walter and his family learn to cope with excessive worrying, and how Walter gains control over his life, are at the heart of this book. It is intended for children and parents to read together. It is equally intended for mental health professionals (psychiatrists, psychologists, clinical social workers and school counselors) and pediatricians to use in their work with those children, ages 6–12, whose worries significantly interfere with their daily functioning. It is based in the principles of cognitive behavioral, relational and family therapies.

The book provides a unique treatment technique identified as "the toolbox." Using a simple shoebox and typical arts and crafts materials, Walter actually builds a toolbox to hold his "tools," which are the cognitive behavioral strategies he learns in order to take control of his worries. He then constructs the tools, which are visual representations of these strategies. As the story progresses, Walter learns first to self-soothe, relax, and organize himself. He is then able to move on to devising ways to tolerate anxiety-producing stimuli. With much practice, desensitization, and exposure, Walter develops a repertoire of strategies that he can use in any situation; he also develops the capacity to create new tools to meet more novel challenges.

The concept of the toolbox is one that I have developed and refined in my clinical practice. It has proven itself to be a highly successful treatment strategy that can be used both by parents and by trained professionals. It provides children with a multisensory experience in developing coping skills. The process of actually "building" the toolbox, and subsequently the tools, is met with great enthusiasm. It incorporates childrens' delight in creative, imaginative play with a visual and tactile sensory experience that facilitates the internalization of the strategies.

Throughout the story, Walter's inner world is shared, as he deals with fear, distress, frustration, and his at times ambivalent determination to improve the quality of his life. His parents begin to address their own issues as well, acknowledging their part in the dynamics that so often occur in anxious families. In the end, his family experiences great hope for Walter's future and for that of the family. Walter acknowledges that his anxiety is something best managed on his own, albeit with the encouragement of an adult support system. Most significantly, he recognizes that he has the capacity to calm, organize and control himself. He is able to express enormous pride in himself and in his abilities, as he begins to live a fuller and more normative life.

Allyson I. Aborn, LCSW

Chapter 1

WALTER WAS A WORRIER. He worried that his mom would be late picking him up at school. He worried that she would wait at the wrong door. He worried that there might be a thunderstorm, even on the most beautiful day. He worried that the lunchroom would smell like tuna fish and old milk, and that he would gag.

Walter was afraid of dogs, though he wanted one more than anything in the whole world. He was afraid that next year's teacher wouldn't let him go to the nurse. When it was bedtime, Walter worried about bad guys breaking into his house and hiding in his closet.

Walter was scared to go to the doctor's office, because he might need a shot. One time, when his parents finally dragged him there, he hid in the toy chest in the waiting room. In a loud whisper, his mom said, "Walter, you are making a scene."

At the beach, Walter always wore flip-flops so he wouldn't step on glass, cut himself, and need stitches. Stitches seemed too much like a shot to him.

When his little sister Jenny threw up after apple picking, Walter worried that he would throw up too. He worried so much that he threw up.

Walter loved to play baseball, but he couldn't go to the ball field because there might be bees. And when he went shopping with his family, Walter worried that the mall would close and they would be locked in. Overnight.

On and on and on went Walter's worries. Sometimes they disappeared, but new ones always came to take their place.

Jenny was not scared of anything. She would jump really high on their parents' bed. She loved sleepovers. Once, she and her best friends, Nicole and

Becca, slept in a tent in the backyard with no grown-ups and only flashlights to protect them. In her room, Jenny slept with the lights off and read scary stories under the covers with her headlamp.

Walter's parents could not figure out why Walter was so worried.

"When I was a child, I didn't worry about anything," Mom told Dad. But now, Walter's mother worried all the time, just like Walter.

"What are you so worried about?" Dad asked Mom.

"I'm worried that Walter will feel worried!" replied Mom, shaking her head at the whole situation.

So, Walter's mom spent her time trying to do things just the way Walter insisted he needed them done. She hoped that would stop Walter from worrying so much.

At school pick-up, Mom would arrive fifteen minutes early and stand right at the red door. When she and Dad went out, she called Walter all the time, before he could start to worry about if they were safe.

When the family went out to dinner, Walter chose the restaurant. He picked the same one every time. That way, he didn't have to worry that a new place wouldn't have anything he liked.

Jenny always said, "That's not fair!" Jenny liked sushi and falafel and the hibachi restaurant where the chef flipped the food into his hat.

In a tired voice, Mom would say, "I know, honey, but it's just not worth the fight."

Walter's mom would stay at birthday parties where no other parents stayed so Walter didn't have to worry that she would be late picking him up. She made playdates for Walter only with kids who didn't have pets, even though that meant he couldn't play with kids he liked, like Matthew and Michael. When Walter heard on the Weather Channel that rain was predicted, his mom would let him stay home from camp so he didn't have to worry about lightning.

Walter's mother told his father that he had to follow Walter's rules too.

"That's ridiculous!" replied his father.

But because he loved Walter and saw how upset Walter could get, he finally said, in a frustrated voice, "OK, fine."

Even so, Walter worried that his dad wouldn't do everything just the way his mom did. At night, he often heard his parents arguing about how to do things "Walter's Way".

Walter had figured out that if he could not get one parent to do what he needed, he could usually get his way with the other one. His parents would be angry with him when they realized what he was doing, but most of the time he was able to get away with it. It was certainly worth a try.

Chapter 2

ONE DAY, WALTER'S Aunt Alice came to visit. She was on a business trip, flying from here to there and back again. Aunt Alice was Mom's sister and a very lot of fun. Everyone liked it when she was around.

On this visit, Aunt Alice noticed that there were even more things the family couldn't do because of Walter's worries than there had been just a few months ago. She didn't like to see the family this way.

At dinner, she said to Walter's mom, "You know what? He's just like you when you were his age."

"No, no, no!" protested Mom. "What are you talking about? I was completely different."

Aunt Alice laughed. She wiggled her finger at Mom. "Remember camp? I went every July, and so did all the kids in the neighborhood—except you. You couldn't even go on a sleepover until you were fifteen."

"True," said Mom, with a big sigh. She turned to Walter and Jenny. "Sometimes I would throw up when Grandpa Dan and Grandma Susie went out at night. Finally they stopped going out, because it upset me so much. I worried alot about Grandma Susie too. I was afraid that she would forget to wear her raincoat and then she would catch cold and maybe even die."

"And what about spiders?" added Aunt Alice. "Remember when you saw a spider on the curtain in your room and had to sleep in a sleeping bag on my floor for two months?"

The stories went on and on. Walter and Jenny listened, all wiggly and giggly, because some of Mom's fears sounded so goofy. It was fun to listen to those stories. And who would be afraid of that stuff anyway?

But then Aunt Alice's face became serious. She looked at Walter.

"Walter," she said, "your mom's worries were as real and scary to her as yours are to you. And even now she has a worry. She is worrying about your being worried. Your dad and Jenny think about your worries too."

Now no one was laughing. It was quiet. Dad looked sad. Mom looked like she might cry. Even Jenny was sitting still. Tick tock, tick tock went the grandfather clock in the hallway. It seemed very loud.

That night, after the kids went to bed, the grown-ups sat talking for a long, long time. Walter liked hearing their voices as he drifted off to sleep. It felt safe. He wished he could feel that way more of the time.

The next day, Mom and Dad talked to Walter while Jenny and Aunt Alice were at soccer practice. They told him they had decided to take him to see a feelings doctor.

"What's a feelings doctor?" Walter asked. He was already frightened that he might have to get a shot.

"A feelings doctor helps children with their worries," said Dad. "When you go to a feelings doctor, you can talk about what is scary to you, what makes you feel afraid. Then the doctor helps you figure out how you can feel safer and less worried."

How do they do that? Walter wondered to himself. Out loud, he said, "OK." He was so tired of being scared all the time.

The first time, Mom and Dad went to meet with Dr. Rose by themselves. Then the next week Walter went with them. The waiting room of Dr. Rose's office had some comfy chairs and a shelf full of children's magazines and puzzles and board games. There were some dinosaurs in a basket on a little round table. Walter wasn't interested in any of these things. He was scared. His cheeks felt hot and it was hard for him to breathe.

When Dr. Rose greeted Walter, he held his dad's hand tightly. She invited him and his parents to come into her office. The room was cozy like someone's living room, and not at all like a doctor's office. Walter sat down on the couch, right between his parents. He didn't want to cry, but he felt like he might. He was scared of what might happen.

"Take a look around, Walter," said Dr. Rose. "You can check out some of the toys."

But Walter was afraid to leave the couch.

Dr. Rose and Mom and Dad started to talk, and after a while Walter felt calm enough to join in. They talked about school and home and friends, and Walter even told Dr. Rose his second-favorite joke.

"What did the 'o' do when it wanted to turn into an '8'"?

"I don't know," she said.

"Put on a belt!" Walter said. He even managed to give her a small smile. But he wasn't ready to tell her something that was special to him, like his #1 very favorite favorite joke. Why should he trust someone he didn't even know?

When it was time for Walter and his parents to leave, Dr. Rose smiled and said, "I think it would be a good idea for us to meet for a while, Walter, so that we can get right to work on these worries that are giving you such a hard time. I'll be seeing your parents also, but at a different time."

Walter felt confused. He wished he could believe that coming to Dr. Rose would make the worries go away, but it just didn't seem possible. He looked at his mom and dad. They both looked more relaxed than when they first came in; it seemed like they felt Dr. Rose could help. He guessed he'd give it a try.

Chapter 3

W HEN WALTER ARRIVED for his third appointment, he was ready to have his dad sit in the waiting room, instead of being with him in the office while he talked to Dr. Rose. Dr. Rose had told Walter that he could decide when he was ready for that to happen, and Walter was glad he had been given the choice.

By then, Dr. Rose and Walter had started to speak about his worries. They had made a Worry List. It was very long. They had numbered the worries, from the big ones to the not-so-big ones. It felt good to write them down.

"Today", Dr. Rose said, "We're going to talk about being brave. We are going to talk about facing your fears."

Walter shook his head.

"How can I ever do that?", he asked.

Dr. Rose explained. "We will practice, a little bit at a time, over and over, facing situations that feel uncomfortable to you. I know it is hard to believe, but after a while you will actually get used to them!"

How could that be? Walter wondered. Get used to bees? Get used to lightning? The dark?

Dr. Rose showed Walter how to make a WORRY METER to rate how worried he felt and to figure out when he needed to do something to calm himself down. This is what it looked like:

WORRY METER

10	- 10. PANIC
9	- 9. OUT OF CONTROL: I NEED HELP
8	- 8. SHAKY; HARD TO BREATHE; HEART RACING; CRYING
7	- 7. SCARED: CAN THINK ONLY ABOUT THE WORRY
6	- 6. STARTING TO FEEL SICK WITH WORRY
5	- 5. BODY FEELING UNCOMFORTABLE
4	- 4. WORRIED BUT IN CONTROL
3	- 3. THINKING ABOUT THE WORRY
2	- 2. TINY BIT WORRIED
1	- 1. CALM

WHAT NUMBER ARE YOU?

Walter described how he felt at the different numbers. At 1 he felt just fine. He felt pretty good at 2 also, although a tiny bit of worry was beginning to creep in. At 3 that "tiny bit" was a little bigger. And at 4 the worry was starting to take up more space in Walter's thoughts. By 5 the worry was beginning to make Walter feel uncomfortable; his cheeks were warm and his palms sweaty. At 6 Walter's cheeks were definitely hot, and the worry was really on his mind. A 7 meant that Walter could not think about anything else, and that he felt very scared. By 8 his heart was beating way too fast. He was having trouble breathing and felt like he might cry. When he reached 9, Walter knew he wasn't able to control the worry; it had taken over and he needed help. At 10, it was too late even to ask for the help: Walter was in a panic, and there was no way he could think straight or do anything to calm himself down.

Dr. Rose said, "You can keep this rating system in your head to use whenever you feel worried. If you're feeling more than a 5, you'll need to act fast to calm down and get back in control of yourself."

"But how can I do that?" Walter asked.

"We already know a lot more about your worries than we did before. We know how you feel when you are worried, and how hard it is to have fun and to pay attention in school. We know that a lot of the worries don't even make much sense, but they are still there."

Dr. Rose continued: "Walter, this is what we have to do. We have to make you be the boss of your worries; your worries cannot be the boss of you. You are going to have to be very, very brave and stand up to those worries and say, 'YOU ARE NOT THE BOSS OF ME!' "

"But how?" Walter persisted. He was feeling even more frustrated.

"By building a toolbox," replied Dr. Rose. "We're going to make a toolbox, and in that toolbox we'll put all kinds of tools you can use to take control of your worries. Grown-ups might call them strategies or techniques, but we're calling them tools. We'll make tools that will help you relax and calm down when you feel very tense. Then we'll make tools you can use for specific worries. You're going to find out that, whatever the situation, you can use one of your tools to help you get through. And if you don't have just the right tool, you can invent a new one."

Chapter 4

THE FOLLOWING WEEK, Walter brought a big shoebox from home. He made handles and decorated it with construction paper and markers and stickers. He wrote "WALTER'S TOOLBOX" in big letters across the top, and on the sides he wrote slogans like "YOU CAN DO IT!" and "WALTER'S POWER PACK." He drew some tools on the outside: hammers and wrenches and even a flashlight, things he had seen his parents use to repair stuff at home. While he worked on the toolbox, he and Dr. Rose talked about how he was feeling and what life was like at home, at school, and with his friends.

Finally Walter said, "My toolbox is ready. Now how do I make the tools?"

Dr. Rose said, "There are lots of different ways. One boy I know made his look like Bob-the-Builder tools. Other kids made theirs in the shapes of animals or makeup or geometric patterns or something to do with the tool itself."

Walter thought hard about making his tools. And then, because he was Walter, he began to worry. How could he carry a toolbox around with him? It would make him look different. Kids certainly wouldn't understand, and they might even laugh at him.

So Dr. Rose told him about the OTHER toolbox. He could not believe what she said next: "The other toolbox, Walter, will be in your head! It will be imaginary. That way you can keep your tools with you all the time."

"You mean a VIRTUAL toolbox?" Walter asked.

"Exactly," Dr. Rose replied.

He had never heard anything so cool: he could take his tools with him wherever he went! And for now, his real toolbox could stay in Dr. Rose's closet or on his desk at home.

Walter and Dr. Rose began by working on tools to help Walter calm down when he felt very upset, when he was more than a 5 on his Worry Meter. She called these RELAX-ATTACK tools.

Dr. Rose explained, "Sometimes you may feel like you can't breathe. Sometimes your heart may pound or your hands and feet may feel all tingly. When you begin to feel changes like these, it could be the beginning of something called a panic attack. Even though panic attacks don't last very long and they can't hurt you, they can feel very scary."

Dr. Rose had several suggestions for what he could try. First, she told Walter that it would help to do some big-time physical activity to get rid of all the energy that his body produced when he was so upset. They came up with a list of things to do:

1. Run up and down the stairs until he couldn't do it anymore.
2. Jump on the trampoline.
3. Run back and forth in the yard or in a safe room in his house.

"Using ice can help too," Dr. Rose added. "You can either rub your face with a wet ice cube, hold wet ice cubes in your hands, or stick your face into some very cold water. I know it sounds weird, but it really works. If you feel like it's hard to breathe, try breathing into a paper bag for a minute or two."

All these things would help to calm down Walter's body and bring him down from the upper numbers on his Worry Meter to a number in the middle.

Then Dr. Rose said, " Now we are ready to talk about what you can do next. DEEP BREATHING is a tool you can use for every worry at every number on the chart, and you can do it wherever you are." She showed Walter how to breathe in very slowly through his nose and out very slowly through his mouth. They counted while they breathed in for five, out for five. In for five, out for five. Walter imagined the air going through his body and helping him to calm down.

Walter was ready to create his very first tools! He decided to draw a big mouth, and he colored it and cut it out. He wrote on it: "TAKE 5 DEEP BREATHS." He put the tool in his toolbox and entered the imaginary tool in the virtual toolbox in his head. His second tool was a giant ice cube, and he wrote on it: "COOL YOURSELF OFF!"

Walter learned lots of other tools to calm himself down. He learned to count slowly to 10. For that tool, he made big bubble numbers, all attached, and colored them in. Then he wrote "COUNT TO 10" on the numbers. He put it in his toolbox.

Next, Dr. Rose taught him how to do CLENCHING AND UNCLENCHING. She asked Walter to lie down in a comfortable position on her couch. "We're going to start at your toes, and you'll relax each part of your body, all the way up to your hair," she said.

Walter clenched his toes very tight and counted to 5 slowly, thinking about how tight and hard they felt. Then he relaxed his toes, and noticed how soft and calm they felt. By the time Walter got to his knees, he could say to himself, "My toes are relaxed, my calves are relaxed, my knees are relaxed,"—and they really did feel different.

Walter said, "I can use this tool when I can't fall asleep."

"True," said Dr. Rose. "And you can also use it in a different way if you're at school or anywhere that other people are around. You can just clench your fists and your toes and then relax them, and no one will ever know that you're calming yourself down."

Walter's tool for relaxing was a picture of himself lying in bed. He wrote on it: "CLENCHING AND UNCLENCHING."

After that, Dr. Rose said, "Walter, now I'm going to show you how to do THE TURTLE. You'll have to do some pretending."

That was just fine with Walter. He liked to pretend.

"Can you show me what a turtle does when it thinks there is danger around?" Dr. Rose asked.

Walter crouched on the floor and pretended he was a turtle. He put his arms and his legs and his imaginary tail inside his shell.

Dr. Rose said, "While you're in there, use your tools to calm yourself."

Walter breathed deeply, and when he felt calm, he came out, one leg at a time, then his arms, and finally his head. They practiced a lot. It helped to have that cooling-down time inside his shell.

His tool was a big turtle; he made moveable arms and legs on it. He wrote on the turtle's back: "DO THE TURTLE!"

For every tool they put into Walter's toolbox, they made that same virtual tool for the imaginary toolbox inside his head. Walter certainly had a lot of new tools!

Chapter 5

E VERY WEEK, WALTER AND DR. ROSE practiced what he was learning, and Walter practiced at home by himself. Once he got the hang of the relax-attack tools, he could feel himself start to calm down. And when Walter felt calmer, he could think more clearly.

He used some tools, like TALK TO MYSELF and TELL A GROWN-UP, very often. For the first, he had drawn a picture of himself with a big talk bubble over his head. It said: "STOP! TALK TO MYSELF." Once he realized that he could talk to himself and change some scary thoughts that automatically came into his head, it became easier and easier to think of things to say to himself that would shrink his worries.

Walter could see that "TALK TO MYSELF" would become one of his most important tools. He could do it anywhere and anytime and no one would even know. He thought about some things he could say to himself when he started to feel worried. He made tools for each of these:

1. "BE BRAVE!"
2. "YOU CAN DO IT!"
3. "THE MORE I TRY IT, THE EASIER IT GETS!"
4. "I AM THE BOSS OF THIS WORRY! IT IS NOT THE BOSS OF ME!"

Walter thought about how to do "TALK TO MYSELF" when he had a special worry. So, when he worried that his mother wasn't in the carpool line, he could say to himself, "Mom tells me when she isn't coming. There are a lot of cars in the line today. I will talk to my friends while I am waiting for her." Or, if he was worried that lightning would strike him at camp, he could say to himself, "If the counselors thought it was dangerous to be outside now, they would bring us inside. It is their job to make sure we are safe."

Walter especially liked the tool he called THINK ABOUT A PEACEFUL PLACE. He imagined himself at Grandpa Dan's little cottage in the country, helping mow the big lawn. He would think about this until he felt calm enough to face what was worrying him. He drew himself floating in Grandpa's pool, looking up at some fluffy clouds.

He learned to use another very important tool, which Dr. Rose called a WORRY CHART.

Dr. Rose said, "Tell me something you worry about."

Walter said, "Thunderstorms." In the column headed "What is the worry?" Walter wrote, "thunderstorms." In the next column, "How do you feel?" Walter wrote, "scared."

Then the chart asked him to rate how strong his feeling was, from 1 to 10. Walter wrote an 8.

The next question was: "What is the worst thing that could happen in this situation?" That was tough; even thinking about thunderstorms could make Walter feel like crying, and his cheeks felt hot. Yet here he was, in this safe office with Dr. Rose and with the sun shining on the floor, and so he wrote, "I'm scared the lightning could hit me and I could die".

"Now comes the most important part of the whole chart," said Dr. Rose. "It's time to write down what you can say or do to change this worry. I can help you figure this out, if you like."

Walter thought for a while. Then he said, "I can be careful not to go swimming if there is lightning and loud thunder. But what else could I do?"

Dr. Rose said, "You could talk to yourself. You know something about lightning. What could you say to yourself?"

Walter wrote down three things he could say to himself:

1. *If there was any danger, the camp would not let me go in the pool.*
2. *People almost never get hit by lightning.*
3. *My camp is fifty years old, and no one has ever been hit by lightning. The camp has a plan for keeping the children safe.*

Dr. Rose asked, "Is there anything else you can do when you start to feel worried about lightning?"

WORRY CHART

Name: Walter

Date: September 16

What is the worry?	Rate your worry 1-10 1= Not worried 10= Most worried	What do you think could happen?	How are you feeling?	What can you do or say to help with the worry?	How do you feel now? Rate your worry 1-10 1= Not worried 10= Most worried
Thunder storms and lightning	8	If the lightning hits my house it will burn down.	nervous, scared, anxious. Like I can't breathe, feel like crying.	①talk to myself. ②Think about something else that I like.	3

Worry Chart 2

3/7/2011

19

"Yes," replied Walter. "I could think about something else."

"Like what?"

"Like what activities we'll do in my bunk if we can't be outside for a while. I can play a game or tell stories or work on an art project."

"Good plan, good tool!" said Dr. Rose.

To finish the chart, Walter rated how he felt now that he had so many tools to deal with lightning and thunder. He put a 3 in that column.

Then Walter made another new tool. THINK ABOUT SOMETHING ELSE was a tool he could use in all kinds of situations. He put it in his big toolbox and his virtual toolbox. Then he made a list of what he could think about instead. His list started slowly, but it quickly grew: Walter had lots of interesting things to think about when he didn't have to spend all his time thinking about his worries.

Even so, Walter's worried thoughts still came into his head. It was what happened afterward that was changing. Now, when he began to worry that his mother might be late because she had been in a car accident, he would say "STOP!" to that thought. Instead, inside his head, he would use his "talk to myself" tool and say, "Mom is a good driver. She has been driving for a long time. If she's late it's because there was traffic or she didn't leave on time."

If Walter was scared that he wouldn't get the right answer when his teacher sent him up to do a math problem on the board, he would say to himself, "STOP! Lots of kids don't get the right answer the first time. That's why we're in school—to learn."

Often, he didn't even need to go to a grown-up for help. More and more, Walter was able to change how he was thinking. His toolbox was filling up.

Chapter 6

O NE WEEK, DR. ROSE gave Walter another idea. She called it the DVD PLAYER.

"Walter," she said, "imagine you have a DVD player in your forehead." She gave him an invisible remote to control the DVD player. "Now pretend to turn it on."

He pressed an imaginary Power button, then Eject.

"OK, now put in any DVD that you want to watch; since they're imaginary, you can pick whatever you want. It can be a favorite episode of a TV show or a favorite movie; it can be a DVD of a fun time you had, like a birthday party or a vacation. Put it in, press Play, and watch that DVD instead of thinking about your worry. If you get tired of the DVD, eject it and put in another."

Walter loved this tool. He made a DVD library and wrote down pages of DVDs he could watch, ranging from the Harry Potter movies to the time his Uncle Billy took him to see the Giants play and he got picked to go onto the field at halftime. He used this tool when he knew he had to think about something else, and he also used it when he could not fall asleep, putting in videos until he drifted off.

Next Dr. Rose taught Walter about the TRAFFIC LIGHT tool. Together they created a big traffic light, with red at the top, green on the bottom, and yellow in between. Dr. Rose said that when Walter felt anxious, he could imagine that traffic light. First, he would imagine the red light turning on.

"Red means STOP," she said. "That means stop the worried thought, and don't let it keep going. Yellow means CALM DOWN, THINK ABOUT THE PROBLEM, AND MAKE A PLAN," Dr. Rose continued. "So you may have to use some other tools first to help you to calm down. Like what, Walter?"

Walter knew what was in his toolbox, so he could answer right away. "Like running up and down the stairs, or breathing, or counting slowly, or clenching and unclenching."

"Great," said Dr. Rose. "Once you are calmer, you can make a plan for what you can do to deal with the problem. Now it's time for the green light. That means GO. You have a plan, and you can go ahead and do it."

They practiced a lot and thought up all sorts of situations where the traffic light would be a good tool to use. Walter told Dr. Rose about Andrew and Emily, the twins who lived next door. Their birthday party was going to be at a restaurant Walter did not know, where there might not be anything Walter liked on the menu.

Walter's first thought was that he would not be able to go, and he felt very sad about that. Andrew and Emily were his really good friends. Then he thought about the traffic light. He saw the red light that meant STOP! He stopped the thought that he couldn't go to the party. Then he went to the yellow light. He thought about the problem and what he could do. He made two plans: First, he would go online with his parents and see if the restaurant had a menu on its website. If it did, he would see right away if there was anything there he wanted to eat. Second, if there wasn't a menu or if he didn't like anything on the menu, he could eat something before the party, and then just have a drink and birthday cake. He was ready for the green light: GO! He had a plan, and his plan meant he could go to his friends' party!

Walter and Dr. Rose made all kinds of other tools too. They would imagine situations where a worry came up, and Walter would practice deciding what tools he could use and how he would handle himself.

Sometimes they would leave the office to practice. On days that looked cloudy, they walked outside, and Walter had to use his tools when he heard thunder. In the spring, they began to work on Walter's fear of bees. Dr. Rose called what they were going to do EXPOSURE THERAPY, because Walter would gradually let himself be exposed to the very things he feared.

The worry about bees was really tough for Walter. He told that to Dr. Rose, so they started very slowly. First, they looked up bees in some insect books

Dr. Rose found in the library. Walter got used to seeing bees, and he learned about their habits. Then they looked on the Internet for videos of bees so Walter could see them in action. They decided to make a journal, where Walter listed the various types of bees, pasted pictures that he had downloaded and printed, and wrote something about each species. They also bought a disposable camera so that when he did eventually see a bee, Walter could photograph it.

Finally the day came when they began to walk outside to look at bees. The first few times, they walked on the streets downtown, not a place where they were likely to see many bees. Walter always brought his camera and his bee journal with him, so that if he did see one he could jot it down by the correct species.

Once he was comfortable walking around, they walked to a neighborhood where there were some gardens. There were bees in the flowers. Although Walter felt frightened, he was able to stay near the gardens long enough to take a picture and note the bees in his journal. Each time he did this, it felt a little less scary.

Finally, once Walter was a little more comfortable, they were ready to go to the big park, where Walter knew there would be lots of bees. It was hard for him to do. He needed to be very, very brave. And he was. He used many of his tools, first to calm himself down and then to change his thoughts. He told himself that he knew that the bees weren't interested in him, they were interested in the pollen. He told himself that as long as he didn't bother the bees, they probably wouldn't bother him. Little by little, he felt more comfortable being outside. More and more, he didn't even think about bees when he went out to play.

Walter continued to keep his Worry Chart with all his worried thoughts, so that he and Dr. Rose could review what he was thinking about and how he handled hard situations. It helped to reread old pages and to see how many new experiences he was having.

Chapter 7

ALL THIS TIME, Walter's parents were meeting with Dr. Rose, who helped them understand more about themselves. Walter's mother recognized that she really was a worrier too, just like Aunt Alice had said.

Walter's father didn't worry the same way as Walter and his mother, but he could see that he had some worries of his own. He liked to get to the airport very, very early, just in case. He needed to close and check all the windows in the house every night, or he couldn't sleep. He had a hard time when he had to do big presentations at work.

His mom and dad talked to Dr. Rose about how they felt when Walter was so worried. Their lives had revolved around his "what ifs." Dr. Rose helped Walter's mother see that when she tried so hard to do what Walter wanted her to do, she wasn't helping him be brave and face his fears. She was helping him avoid them.

His parents began to understand better how Walter felt. After that, they weren't so frustrated with him, and they became more patient. They would say to Walter, "I know this is really hard for you," and Walter could tell they really meant it.

Walter's parents learned about his tools and how they could help Walter use them. They often came to his appointments with Dr. Rose so they could practice with him. Even though they didn't build a toolbox, they worked on their own tools to use when Walter was having a hard time.

Dr. Rose helped Mom and Dad understand how important it was that Walter face his fears, a bit at a time, and over and over again, until those experiences were just as ordinary as getting up in the morning or eating dinner. This took lots of bravery on his part and lots of patience on theirs.

Many times, Dr. Rose gave the whole family "homework" to do, like taking Walter to a pet store to get used to being with dogs, or very gradually going to places where there might be bees. They started to use a chart for these projects, and Walter could earn things he really wanted if he was able to do what was listed on the chart. Here is what Walter's chart looks like:

Walter and his parents talked a lot about the rewards he could earn. If Walter earned enough checks on his chart, each week he could choose to go to the playground with the skateboarding ramps, or get a pack of baseball cards, or stay up later one night of the weekend. They made the chart like a legal contract; Mom, Dad, Walter, and Dr. Rose all signed it. That meant they all agreed to what they were working on and to what Walter could earn.

Life was changing at home. When Walter felt worried, one of his parents would say, "OK, Walter, you have to be very brave now. Figure out how to calm down. Then decide what tools you are going to pull from your toolbox and get to work."

And Walter did get to work. So did his parents. His mom tried very hard not to automatically take care of everything so that he wouldn't get worried. Both his parents were very nice but very firm about Walter doing more activities. Mom said, "Yes, Walter, you are going on the class trip to the Marshlands, on the bus," and Dad said, "Yes, Walter, you are going to Kevin's party, even if he has a dog, two cats, and a very large iguana."

It helped Walter that he couldn't avoid these activities, because when he actually did them he had a great time. It helped Walter, too, that his parents weren't arguing all the time about what he could and could not do. Or if they were, it wasn't happening in front of him. It was much harder for him to get one to say yes if the other said no. After a while, he gave up even trying that old trick.

Life still felt scary sometimes, but Walter knew what he needed to do to feel more comfortable. He took his virtual toolbox with him wherever he went. Looking at him, no one even knew he had his tools, but they were there all the time. It became so automatic to use his tools, or to make new tools, that he often just did it without even noticing.

He did more and more, he played more and more, and he felt more and more in control of what happened to him. Gradually, he visited Dr. Rose less often, until they finally just had a "check-up" every few months.

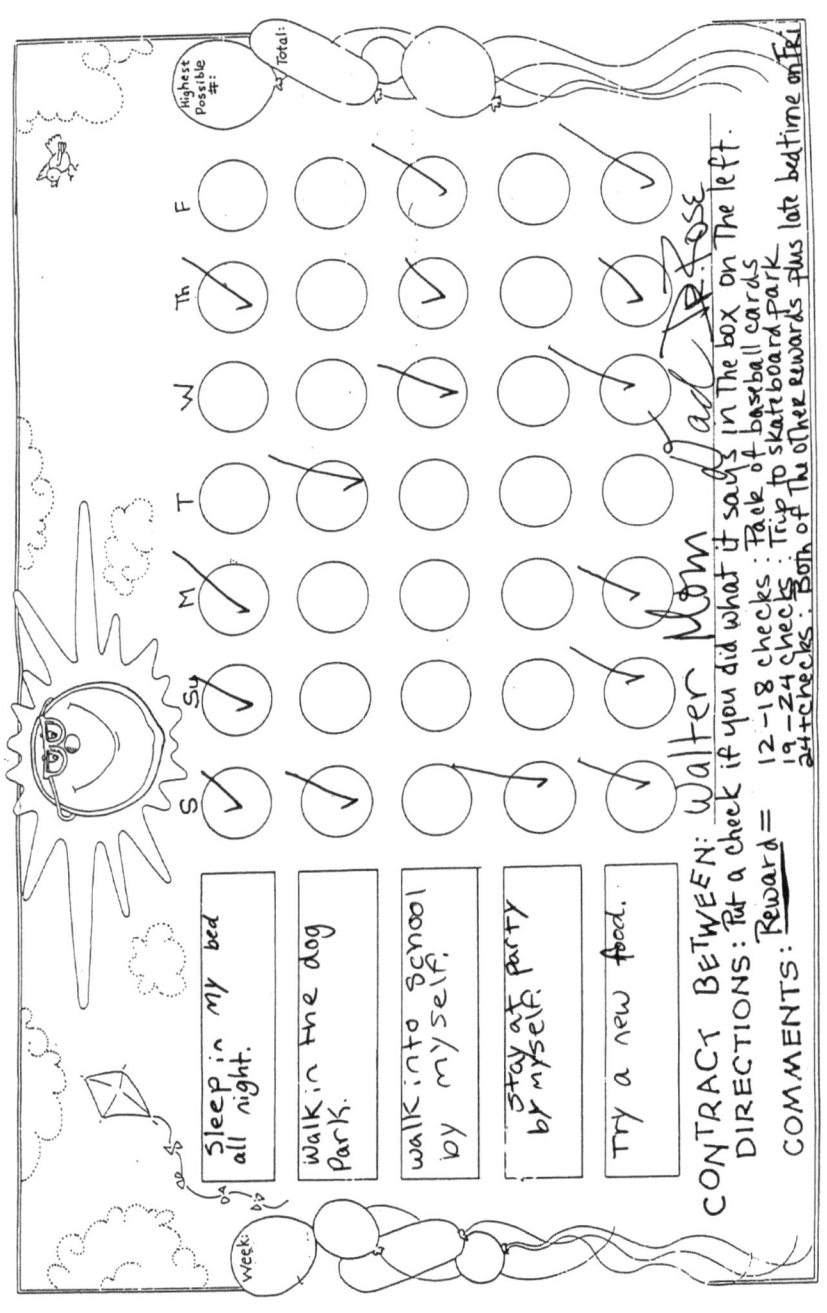

Highest Possible #:

Total:

week:

	S	Su	M	T	W	Th	F

Sleep in my bed all night.

Walk in the dog park.

Walk into school by myself.

Stay at party by myself.

Try a new food.

CONTRACT BETWEEN: Walter Mom Dad R Rose
DIRECTIONS: Put a check if you did what it says in the box on the left.
Reward = 12–18 checks: Pack of baseball cards
19–24 checks: Trip to skateboard park
24+checks: Both of the other rewards plus late bedtime on Fri
COMMENTS:

The next time Aunt Alice came to visit, everyone in the family was talking at the same time about how life was different in their house. Aunt Alice could see the difference; she didn't need them to tell her. She was so proud of Walter. Mom and Dad were so proud of Walter too. And Jenny was so happy that Walter wanted to walk home from school with her and to jump on the bed with her and could sleep in his room with the lights out. Maybe someday he would even spend the night with her outside in the tent (with a headlamp, of course).

Best of all, Walter was proud of Walter! "I am the boss of me!" he said, with a big smile, his toolbox in his hand.

Appendix

Sample Toolboxes

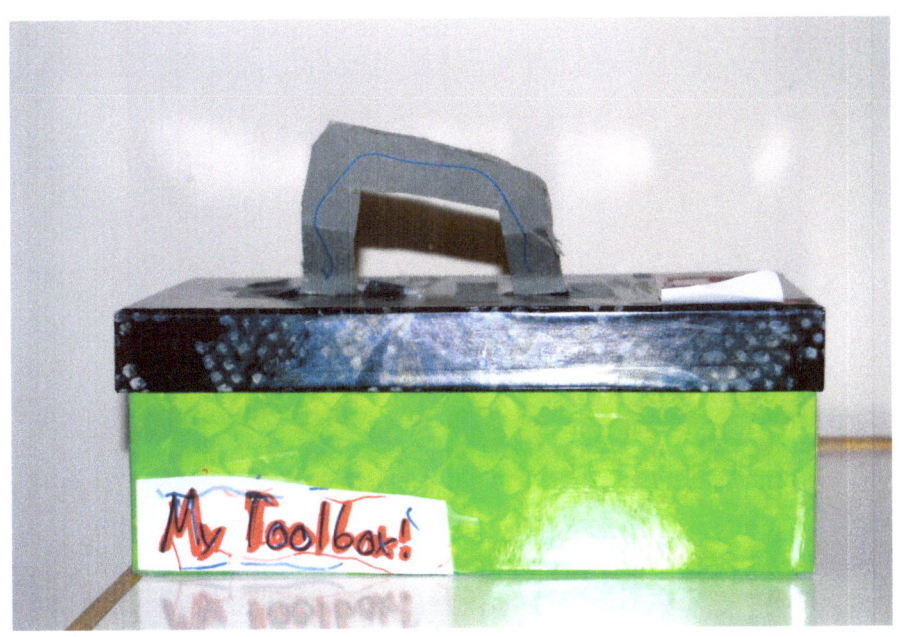

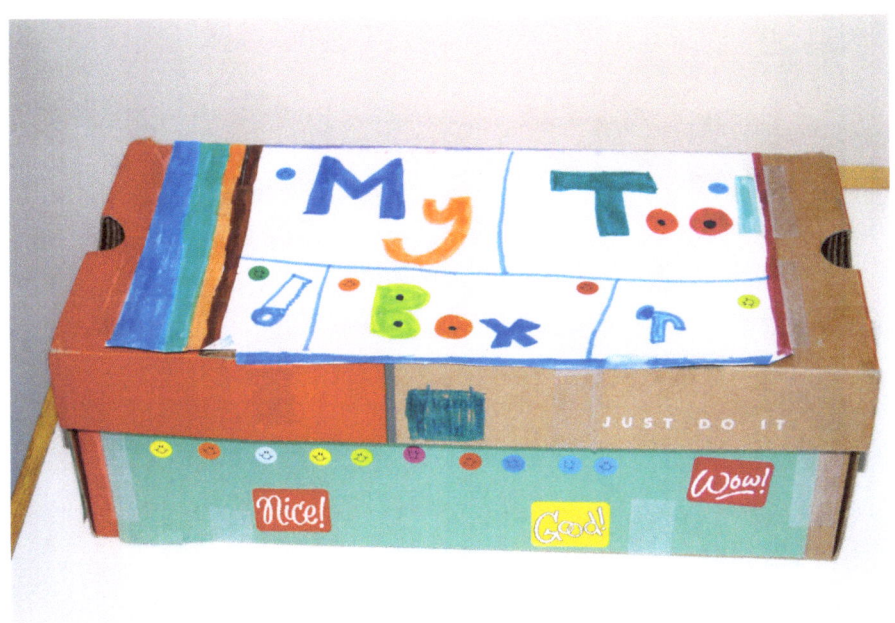

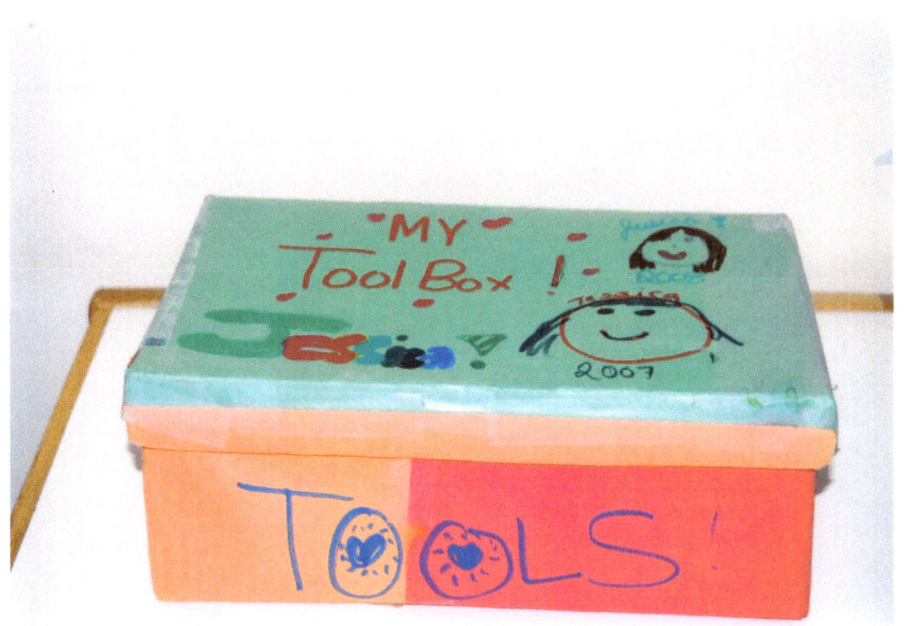

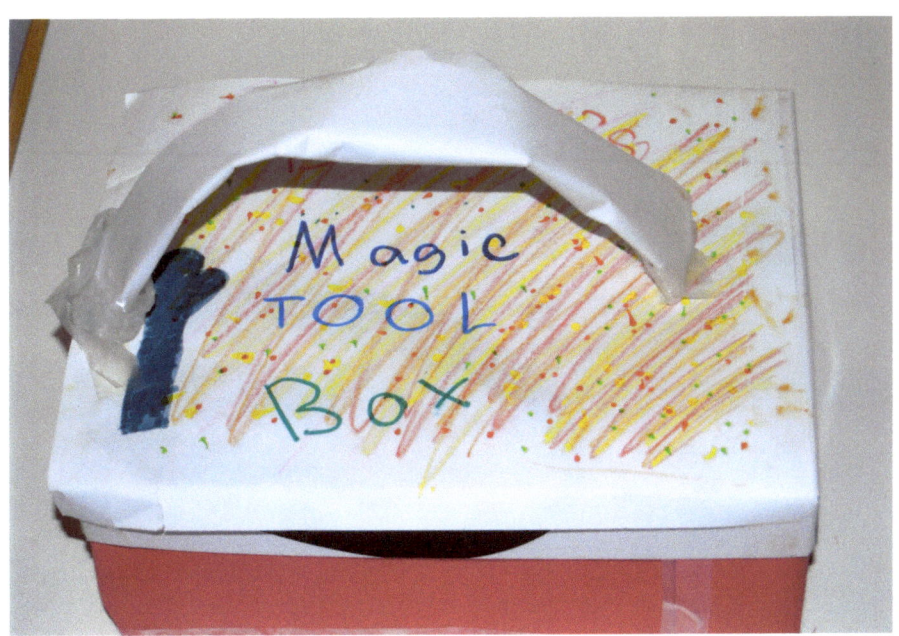

Sample Tools

Sample Worry Chart

WORRY CHART
Allyson Aborn LCSW

Name: _____   Date _____

What do you worry about?	Rate your worry 1-10 1= Not worried 10= Most worried	What do you think would happen?	What are you feeling?	What can you do or say to help with the worry?	How do you feel now? Rate your worry 1-10 1= Not worried 10= Most worried

Worry Chart 2   10/22/2007

Download this chart at:
www.waltertheworrier.com

39

Sample Behavior Goals Chart

Download this chart at:
www.waltertheworrier.com

www.ingramcontent.com/pod-product-compliance
Lightning Source LLC
Chambersburg PA
CBHW050834290526
45792CB00001B/388